Instant CloudFlare Starter

A practical guide for using CloudFlare to effectively secure and speed up your website

Jeff Dickey

PUBLISHING

BIRMINGHAM - MUMBAI

Instant CloudFlare Starter

First published: June 2013

Production Reference: 1300513

Published by Packt Publishing Ltd.
Livery Place
35 Livery Street
Birmingham B3 2PB, UK.

ISBN 978-1-78216-028-1

www.packtpub.com

Credits

Author

Jeff Dickey

Reviewers

Eric Glasser

Ayesh Karunaratne

Acquisition Editor

Erol Staveley

Commissioning Editor

Harsha Bharwani

Technical Editors

Saumya Kunder

Amit Ramadas

Project Coordinator

Amigya Khurana

Proofreader

Aaron Nash

Production Coordinator

Melwyn D'sa

Cover Work

Melwyn D'sa

Cover Image

Conidon Miranda

About the Author

Jeff Dickey is a San Francisco based web/mobile engineer. He's worked with various firms and startups to build products and scale platforms. Currently he is working with Tapjoy, scaling one of the largest Rails platforms in the world. He also advises startup firms on how best to design their architecture, structure their teams, and manage their projects.

He is active in the open source community and has provided contributions to various projects, including Ruby on Rails. He also writes on his blog at `http://dickey.xxx`.

About the Reviewers

Eric Glasser graduated from Vanderbilt University with a degree in Engineering Science after three years as a junior. Within Engineering Science, Eric focused on technology and systems development. During his last two years at Vanderbilt, Eric started a company called Virtual Newsroom, based around building a process and content management system for newspapers called Virtual Newsroom. After releasing Virtual Newsroom as an open source project Eric started a web development and consulting company working with small and medium-sized businesses. For the last year Eric has operated his web development business managing both local and outsourced teams of developers. Eric also worked with an angel investor at their startup company "Launch.it" as a technology specialist in New York. Eric has experienced working a wide variety of companies, and the challenges of both starting and operating a business.

Ayesh Karunaratne is a freelance PHP/Drupal web developer from Kandy, Sri Lanka. He is currently following a Bachelor's degree in Computer Science from University of Colombo.

He has more than four years of experience in PHP, and he has been involved in many PHP related websites as a backend developer, performance analyst, security reviewer, and architectural designer. He has taken part in one of the most appreciated e-government solutions in the United States. He is also the leader of Drupal Sinhalese translation team to bring Drupal to native Sinhala-speaking people in Sri Lanka.

He also spends his leisure time writing blog posts about web development and freelancing tips. Apart from his technical interests, he loves swimming, hanging out with friends, hiking, and watching movies.

> I would like to thank my parents and all my friends who helped me to review this book with suggestions and improvements to be considered. It was a great experience to work with Packt.

www.packtpub.com

Support files, eBooks, discount offers, and more

You might want to visit www.packtpub.com for support files and downloads related to your book.

Did you know that Packt offers eBook versions of every book published, with PDF and ePub files available? You can upgrade to the eBook version at www.packtpub.com and as a print book customer, you are entitled to a discount on the eBook copy. Get in touch with us at service@packtpub.com for more details.

At www.packtpub.com, you can also read a collection of free technical articles, sign up for a range of free newsletters and receive exclusive discounts and offers on Packt books and eBooks.

packtlib.packtpub.com

Do you need instant solutions to your IT questions? PacktLib is Packt's online digital book library. Here, you can access, read and search across Packt's entire library of books.

Why Subscribe?

- ✦ Fully searchable across every book published by Packt
- ✦ Copy and paste, print and bookmark content
- ✦ On demand and accessible via web browser

Free Access for Packt account holders

If you have an account with Packt at www.packtpub.com, you can use this to access PacktLib today and view nine entirely free books. Simply use your login credentials for immediate access.

Table of Contents

Instant CloudFlare Starter

Welcome to *Instant CloudFlare Starter*. This book has been especially created to provide you with all the information that you need to get set up with CloudFlare. You will learn the basics of CloudFlare, make your site perform faster, and discover some tips and tricks for using CloudFlare.

This document contains the following sections:

So, what is CloudFlare? looks at what CloudFlare actually is, what you can do with it, and why it's so great.

Installation teaches you how to set up CloudFlare with the minimum fuss so that you can use it as soon as possible.

Quick start shows you how to perform one of the core tasks of CloudFlare—making your site work faster. By following these steps you will learn how to configure your site with CloudFlare enhancements, which will be the basis of most of your work in CloudFlare.

Top 5 features you need to know about explains how to perform five tasks with the most important security features of CloudFlare. By the end of this section you will be able to secure your site with CloudFlare. Also, CloudFlare offers an extensive array of apps for you to use. These apps can help make your site perform faster, be more secure, offer a better user experience, and discover analytics.

People and places you should get to know provides you with many useful links to the CloudFlare pages, as well as a number of helpful articles, tutorials, blogs, and Twitter feeds.

So, what is CloudFlare?

CloudFlare is a service that webmasters can use to provide better performance and higher security on their websites. High performance websites lead to higher visitor engagement, retention, and conversions. CloudFlare has various tools to help speed up your website. Usually the best way to increase a website's performance is with a **Content Delivery Network** (**CDN**). In order to understand how CloudFlare optimizes the performance, it's important to first understand how a CDN works.

A CDN is a distributed network of servers that is generally used to deliver static content. A CDN will be distributed on servers throughout the world. CDNs are also optimized to provide static content with proper software and network topologies. A common way in which this is leveraged in many web applications to deliver a dynamic HTML page is through an application server, then deliver the images, CSS, and JavaScript through a CDN.

This allows the content to be served up quickly as the servers are located closer to the end user. It also helps distribute the load off the application servers, thus making the experience for end users better as well as saving server resources. It's an important part of any website. If you want your website to load fast and scale well, then it's a necessity.

In order to understand the difference between CloudFlare and a traditional CDN, you should know that CloudFlare is not a traditional CDN. A more traditional CDN would be a service such as CloudFront, EdgeCast, or Akamai. In these systems, you would have a CDN to mirror your content. Unfortunately, this approach requires the CDN to know when the content is updated, and be able to separate the dynamic content from the static content.

Typically, the way this works is when a file is requested through the CDN (say an image), the browser will request it from the CDN. If the CDN does not have a copy of the file, it will request it from the origin host (your web server). It is then cached for all future requests. If the file changes, it needs to be explicitly invalidated either manually or as a deploy process. Otherwise it will eventually expire. This requires a fair amount of backend programming to use effectively.

CloudFlare handles this problem for you by running all content through the CDN and it internally figures out what needs to be cached through the CDN and what doesn't. This means CloudFlare is very easy to set up.

The biggest difference between CloudFlare and other CDNs is that CloudFlare serves every request through the site. Other CDNs only serve static content. This allows CloudFlare to optimize much further.

The analytics and apps are able to do this because they act as a proxy between the application server and the user. After the server generates a response, CloudFlare will alter it to include the new functionality that you've added. For example, if you wanted to add Google Analytics through CloudFlare.

Google Analytics requires a bit of JavaScript on the page. CloudFlare can insert this automatically without any server changes through its app functionality.

Before the Google Analytics app is enabled, the server might respond with a page like the following :

```
<html>
   <title>My site</title>
<head>
<body>
   <p>This is my content</p>
</body>
</html>
```

After enabling Google Analytics through CloudFlare, it will modify the response to be like the following:

```
<html>
   <title>My site</title>
<script type="text/javascript">
   var _gaq = _gaq || [];
   _gaq.push(['_setAccount', 'UA-00000000-1']);
   _gaq.push(['_trackPageview']);
   (function() {
      var ga = document.createElement('script'); ga.type = 'text/
javascript'; ga.async = true;
      ga.src = ('https:' == document.location.protocol ? 'https://ssl' :
'http://www') + '.google-analytics.com/ga.js';
      var s = document.getElementsByTagName('script')[0]; s.parentNode.
insertBefore(ga, s);
   })();
</script>
<head>
<body>
   <p>This is my content</p>
</body>
</html>
```

As you can see, the Google Analytics code is injected straight into the response. This allows CloudFlare to be very flexible in changing the location of assets as well. CloudFlare has a variety of other techniques that can be enabled to optimize a website, such as the following:

- **SPDY support**: SPDY is a new protocol designed to be much faster than HTTP at transporting web content.

- **Railgun**: This is a compressor used to reduce the data needed to deliver content.

- **Preloading**: CloudFlare can be configured to preload content that's used often before the user reaches a page that requires it.

- **Rocket Loader**: This ensures that loading external resources doesn't pause the loading of the rest of the page. It can also be configured to combine multiple JavaScript and CSS files into one.

- **AutoMinify**: This compresses HTML, CSS, and JavaScript to reduce file size and improve client-side performance.

- **Local storage caching**: This leverages the browser's local storage to be used as a local cache for objects.

- **Cache header optimization**: This adjusts cache information on request, so browsers will correctly cache the content.

- **Aggressive GZIP**: GZIP compresses data across a network. Some gateways and firewalls will incorrectly notify upstream servers that GZIP is not supported. CloudFlare works despite this and ensures that GZIP is supported where it is available.

- **Browser optimization**: This ensures that images and content are served in the most efficient way possible. For instance, serving images specific to mobile only when accessed by a mobile device.

- **Page prerendering**: This starts loading a new page when hovering over links to them.

It's a long list, but it's important to understand that these optimizations are what CloudFlare does to make your site faster.

CloudFlare watches over many websites across the Internet; if it detects malicious traffic from certain places, it will work to protect sites from attackers in those locations:

- **Denial of Service protection**: When a web server is sent a request, the web server will work on a response and then deliver it to the user. Attackers can take advantage of this by requesting the same content over and over again without listening to the response. This can cripple a system very easily. If CloudFlare detects that this is happening, it will require the user to enter a captcha to continue browsing the website (which a bot will be unable to pass). Since CloudFlare is between the user and your website, this traffic will never hit your site.

- **Other threats**: CloudFlare also monitors for cross-site scripting and SQL injection attacks. There are extensions that we can enable to protect against comment spam and e-mail harvesters as well. CloudFlare can check against browser integrity. This means they will analyze the HTTP requests to see if the headers contain headers associated with malicious actions. There can also be explicit IP address blocks in order to ban some ranges or countries from accessing a website.

- **SSL**: Any website that uses logins/sessions needs to be behind SSL. Without using SSL security, it is easy to hijack a user's session on a public Wi-Fi network, by allowing an attacker to pretend to be a different user. CloudFlare has some tools to easily enable some basic SSL protection for your users. For more information on how this attack is done, read up on the Firesheep exploit at `http:// en.wikipedia.org/wiki/Firesheep`.

- **Blacklisting**: CloudFlare has a database of IP ranges that are known to be harmful traffic. CloudFlare can be enabled to prevent users from these IP addresses from reaching your site without passing a captcha.

CloudFlare allows you to see some analytics information that would be difficult to see otherwise. Analytics services such as Google Analytics, Piwik, or Clicky work by executing JavaScript in the browser. After a page loads, some JavaScript code on the page will send a notification to the analytics service informing about the traffic view. This can easily be blocked by the user and also won't function if JavaScript is disabled. It also will not show bot traffic as they rarely have JavaScript enabled.

There are also tools available to track traffic without JavaScript, such as Webalizer and AWStats. These work by analyzing server logs to report traffic data, and require some software installation on your server.

Often, it can be cumbersome to have engineers add in services to an application such as Typekit or Google Analytics. CloudFlare has a marketplace of apps that can be installed to an application without deployment or changing code on the servers.

Not having to change the code to put an app onto a site lets you to easily try out new analytics, advertising, and social tools.

It's also safe because CloudFlare ensures that the apps are safe and won't cause issues on your site. If you try to enable two conflicting apps, the console will protect you from making that change.

As you can see, CloudFront is more than a traditional CDN. This does not mean that it will solve all scaling problems, but it will solve many of the easier scaling issues with little effort. The security, analytics, and apps functionality are some nice additions to enhance your website as well.

Installation

In order to use CloudFlare, you'll need to have a domain and also the access to change the DNS nameservers for it. It should not result in any downtime for your site.

First, we will add the site in CloudFlare and let it scan our DNS entries. After that completes, we will have to ensure that the DNS entries are valid by cross-referencing with our current DNS server. Finally, we will move the nameservers over to CloudFlare.

For this example, I'll be moving my domain `letsgrababeer.com` over to CloudFlare.

Step 1 – getting CloudFlare set up

Getting CloudFlare set up is pretty simple as compared to most DNS providers. However, the terms used on the Internet to describe DNS are old, and as such, not the easiest to digest when you're new to them. The following are the important concepts behind DNS:

- **IP address**: IP addresses are numeric addresses for computers. It's similar to a street address, and it tells computers where other computers are. When you go to any site, it's through an IP address. They usually look something like this: 74.125.224.72. In fact, that's actually Google's IP address; try typing it into your browser.

- **Domain Name System** (**DNS**): DNS describes the entire process of making domain names route to IP addresses. For example, how `www.google.com` becomes 74.125.224.72.

- **Nameserver**: This is a part of the DNS system that routes domain names to their IP addresses.

- **Domain name registrar**: This is the server that tells us which nameservers are used with what domain. This is different than the nameserver. In our case, the domain name registrar will be the place we registered the domain (GoDaddy, Namecheap, and so on) and the nameserver will be CloudFlare.

- **DNS record**: This is an individual part of a domain's DNS. DNS records allow you to have things like subdomains (for example, `plus.google.com` points to a different server than `www.google.com`). It also allows you to have an e-mail on the same domain as a website. The following is a list of the most common DNS record types:
  - **A record**: It uses a name to point to a specific IP address (for `www.google.com` it is 74.125.224.72)
  - **CNAME record**: This points a name to another name (for `www.google.com` it is google.com)

- ° **Mail Exchanger (MX) record**: This defines whether a mail server needs to receive any e-mails sent to the domain.
- ° **Zone file**: This is a list of DNS records. In our case, CloudFlare will contain the zone file for our domain.
- **Time To Live** (TTL): It defines how long a computer should remember a DNS record before asking again.
- **Text (TXT)**: This is often used to add verification codes, anti-spam techniques, and other arbitrary text. It doesn't affect the domain's connectivity.

The following statement is from the RFC that defined the Internet Protocol:

> *A name indicates what we seek. An address indicates where it is. A route indicates how to get there. [RFC 791]*

Step 2 – adding DNS information to CloudFlare

First create a CloudFlare account at `www.cloudflare.com`. Also, log in to your DNS provider and go to the DNS configuration page. This is most likely your domain registrar (GoDaddy, Namecheap, and so on), unless you have changed it. On my current DNS provider (Namecheap), this is the **All Host Records** tab. You should see things like A, CNAME, and MX records.

Begin the DNS transfer at `https://www.cloudflare.com/my-websites`. Fill in the textbox with your domain name and click on **Add website**:

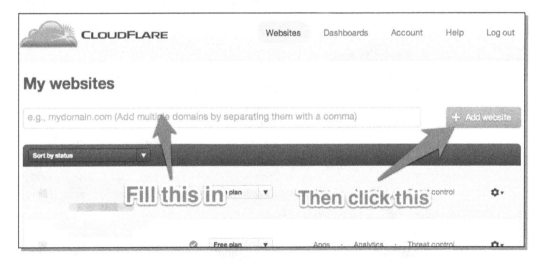

Now CloudFlare is doing a scan of your DNS information so that it will be able to serve the traffic from CloudFlare's nameservers:

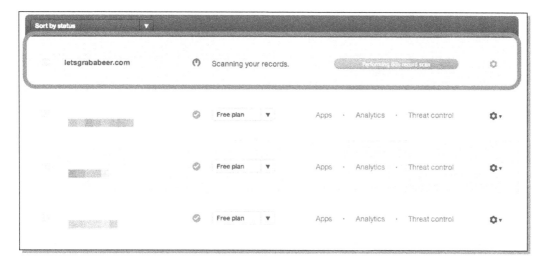

Click on **Continue setup** once that is completed.

Step 3 – verifying DNS configuration

You will now be at the DNS configuration screen:

CloudFlare has grabbed all your DNS records from your current host. We call this a zone file. Each row here represents a different DNS record. Let's take a moment to analyze what each column of this table means:

- **Type**: DNS record type (**A, CNAME, MX,** or **TXT**)
- **Name**: The subdomain that will match to that record

- **Value**: When a client requests a given name, this is the response they will receive. In the case of an A record, for example, it will return the IP address of the website.

- **TTL**: Time to live defines how long the client will cache the record. **Automatic** is usually best here.

- **Active**: This defines whether the request will be routed through CloudFlare for optimization or not.

Let me also bring up my current DNS configuration on my domain registrar. Here, we use Namecheap, so yours will look different depending on which you're currently with:

You'll see that this zone file is very simple. If it had more than just a single A record, I would want to make sure that it is included in CloudFlare's zone file before we switch over to use CloudFlare.

What is interesting here is that there are a few records that I have not specified in my old zone file that CloudFlare has added. They are as follows:

- **direct**: CloudFlare provides a direct subdomain to access your site. This can be helpful in case you're having issues with CloudFlare. If I were to access `direct.letsgrababeer.com` instead of `letsgrababeer.com`, I would be directly accessing my site without going through CloudFlare. This can be helpful if you need to use FTP or for debugging.

- **www**: This CNAME allows users to access `letsgrababeer.com` through `www.letsgrababeer.com` as well. It works like a redirect by saying that anything requesting www will receive the A record.

- **mx**: Since there was no mail server, CloudFlare added this record to allow mail to be received by the same web server at the A record.

And that's it!!

Once you verify that all the records are contained in the new DNS configuration and are set correctly, click on **Continue**.

Quick start – configuring CloudFlare features

Now that we have the DNS configured in CloudFlare, we can enable the features that CloudFlare provides.

Step 1 – configuring initial settings

We'll be welcomed with a screen allowing us to set some initial settings.

I suggest setting **Performance** to **CDN only (safest)** at first, and **Security** to **Medium**. Feel free to read through the various options to decide what you would like. The reason I suggest the lowest level of performance is that you don't yet know how your site will react to CloudFlare. Click on **Continue** when done.

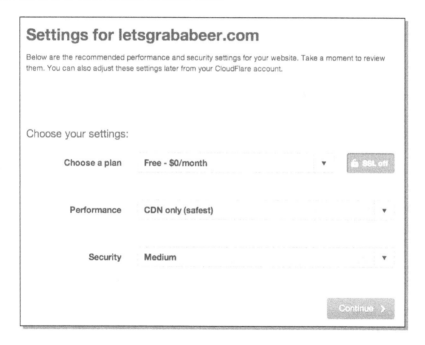

Step 2 – switching nameservers to CloudFlare

Now we are at the step where we need to change our domain registrar's nameserver settings over to CloudFlare. You'll see a screen similar to the following screenshot:

Now I need to go to my registrar and set the nameservers to **anna.ns.cloudflare.com** and **dave.ns.cloudflare.com**.

The nameservers that CloudFlare needs you to use may be different from mine:

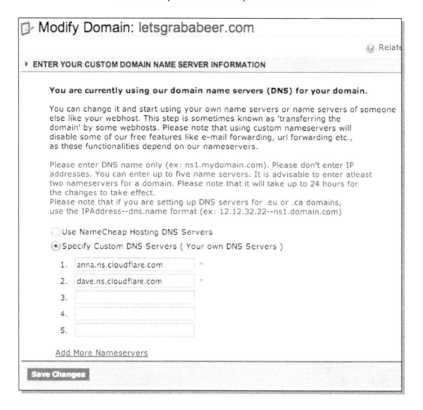

And that's it.

You should receive an e-mail when the nameservers are transferred. It might take up to 24 hours, but it usually happens within a couple of minutes.

To check if your site is working, I suggest the Claire plugin for Google Chrome. It will show an icon when you're browsing a CloudFlare site at `https://chrome.google.com/webstore/detail/fgbpcgddpmjmamlibbaobboigaijnmkl`.

It should turn orange if the site has CloudFlare enabled, along with the features that it is using. Here it is for me on `letsgrababeer.com`:

Step 3 – configuring performance settings

Now that we've got CloudFlare up and running, let's take a look at the performance settings and figure out how to tune them best for your site. To get to the performance settings page, go to **CloudFlare settings** on your CloudFlare dashboard:

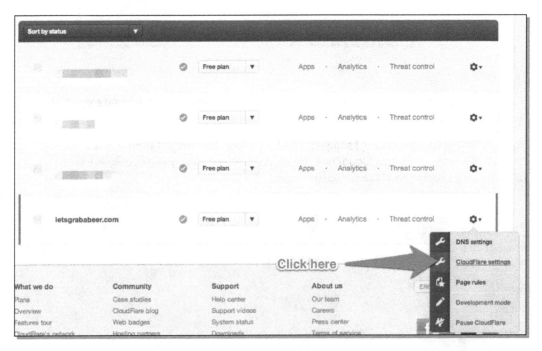

Now click on the **Performance settings** tab to see the different options available to you.

The first option you'll see on this page is the **Performance profile** setting:

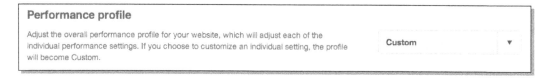

I don't recommend you to use this setting. This will set the individual settings, shown in the following screenshot, to either have a more aggressive caching profile, or a more stable profile. I suggest you read each of the individual settings and set them to what will work for your website instead.

Caching levels

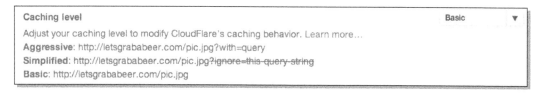

The caching level will adjust the types of static assets that will be cached on your website. Static assets include JavaScript, CSS, and images. There are three levels, basic, aggressive, and simplified:

- **Basic caching**: This only caches assets without a query string. (For example, `http://ipadevice.com/pic.jpg` would be cached but `http://ipadevice.com/pic.jpg?with=query` would never be cached.)

- **Aggressive caching**: This caches assets with a query string. Assets with different query strings should be considered different. (For example, `http://ipadevice.com/pic.jpg?with=query1` would be cached as well as `http://ipadevice.com/pic.jpg?with=query2` would be cached differently.)

- **Simplified caching**: This caches assets with a query string, however ignores the contents of the query string. (For example, `http://ipadevice.com/pic.jpg?with=query1` would be cached and `http://ipadevice.com/pic.jpg?with=query2` would be cached equally.)

I think it is a confusing naming convention because simplified is more aggressive than aggressive is. The query string will be completely ignored under simplified, whereas the aggressive mode will store different versions for different query strings.

To find out if your assets use a query string, open up the **Resources** tab of **Developer Tools** in Google Chrome and reload your page. If you see any query strings, you will probably want aggressive or simplified caching.

If you can, use simplified caching. I'm not sure exactly how CloudFlare's caching works, but usually when caching has to take query strings into account, it will slow down considerably.

Caching TTL

The caching TTL defines how long the static assets will be cached. If your assets change frequently, you'll want this to be low. This is because users will have old assets until TTL is updated. A high TTL will result in a faster experience for your users.

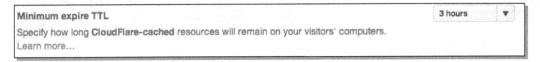

If your static assets never change, keep this high. You can change filenames, or add a query string (depending on the caching level).

The best approach to this is to have some kind of cache busting strategy. That is out of the scope of this book, as it would require server-level changes. However, proper cache busting allows for unlimited caching TTLs.

Asset minification

Minification is the process of stripping unnecessary content out of JavaScript, CSS, and HTML. In some cases, it can dramatically reduce the file size of the assets, improving performance immensely.

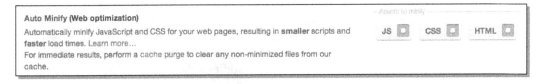

You should not enable this unless you're minifying the assets before they reach CloudFlare. This can potentially cause some issues if the code is written badly. For example, if JavaScript is written without semicolons, sometimes minifying will cause errors in JavaScript. The code would have to be pretty bad for that to happen, so I would still try enabling it unless issues come as a result of it.

You'll need to do a cache purge in order to see the immediate effects of enabling these settings. Cache purge, in simple terms, means clearing the cached copies of assets. So if I clear the cache some time, CloudFlare will have to get original files from the server to serve further page requests.

Rocket Loader

When a web page is loaded, and if there is a JavaScript file, the page will immediately stop rendering and loading until the file is downloaded and run. This damages performance as the page could pipeline much of the loading time:

Rocket Loader instead loads all the JavaScript files asynchronously. This can improve performance by quite a bit. CloudFlare reports a page load time of 12 seconds down to 2 seconds. This also increases the page's `window.onload` time, improving your Google search ranking.

The downsides of enabling this are that (as of writing this book) it is a beta feature, which may cause issues. It also might cause flickering on page load, depending on how JavaScript-heavy a site is, and how exactly it is structured.

Website preloader

The website preloader is a pro feature that downloads static assets before they are required. It analyzes the most commonly accessed content from a website, and if it is not on the current page, it reaches out to ensure that the content will be available for subsequent requests:

There is little downside with this aside from potentially having your users download unnecessary content. This would happen asynchronously, so it would not significantly hurt performance, but would increase server costs.

How much of a benefit this provides will depend on how your site is structured.

Step 4 – configuring e-mail

Now that we have the website working, let's get our e-mail configured. If you don't need e-mail on your domain, you can skip this section.

If you don't currently have a mail server configured, the easiest way to do so is by setting up Google Apps for domains. At the time of writing this book, Google offers a free plan for up to 10 users.

Follow the instructions for your mail provider, and then ensure that your MX records are set appropriately in CloudFlare's zone file. Once you do that, there are a couple other configuration steps you will need to complete in order to ensure deliverability.

Deliverability is a measure of how likely it is for e-mails that are sent from your domain to get stuck in spam filters. The best two ways to ensure that it does not happen is by setting your SPF and DKIM records appropriately.

Sender Policy Framework (SPF) records

At e-mail's core, it cannot validate who has been sent a message. The **from** field can actually be edited to be any e-mail address. A method of verifying the "from" address of an e-mail is by using SPF records.

When you send an e-mail, you can allow recipients to validate that the e-mail came from a valid sender. If you were using Gmail, for example, it would mean that Gmail sends someone an e-mail, purporting from your domain. SPF records allow the client to check and see what hosts are allowed to send e-mail from that domain.

In other words, an SPF record says that if an e-mail gets sent with an @mydomain.com address and did not come from Google, it is probably not me. If there is no match, the e-mail is very likely to end up in a spam box.

SPF records are pretty easy to set up; you'll have to look up your e-mail provider to see what the required SPF record is. For Gmail, it will be: `v=spf1 include:_spf.google.com ~all`. Just go ahead and add that to your DNS configuration in CloudFlare like so:

Definitely set that up to avoid the e-mails that you send from ending up in spam filters.

This paragraph, technically, seems to be incorrect. SPF records, in my opinion, are out of the scope of this book. If the user has an SPF record, let's tell them to add it here. Or a link to learn more about SPF records would be enough I think.

DKIM (DomainKeys Identified Mail)

SPF records are one way by which a recipient can verify a "from" address, but it's only a partial solution. Basically what you're saying is any e-mail sent from Gmail is legitimate. There are a lot of Gmail customers, so that's not even close to a full solution.

DKIM keys allow you to say that only part of the e-mail sent from an e-mail server is a valid e-mail. They work by signing every outgoing e-mail with a digital signature. Recipients can take that signature and verify that it's valid by checking your domain's DKIM records. A side benefit is that this also ensures that the e-mail has not been tampered with along the way.

Not all e-mail providers support DKIM. If you're using Gmail, follow these steps to get a DKIM key: `http://support.google.com/a/bin/answer.py?hl=en&answer=174124`.

Once you get a key, set the key in your CloudFlare DNS configuration:

DKIM records are a little more work to set up than SPF records, but I still recommend using them to ensure deliverability of your e-mail.

Top 5 features you need to know about

Here we will go over the various security, performance, and monitoring features CloudFlare has to offer.

Malicious traffic

Any website is susceptible to attacks from malicious traffic. Some attacks might try to take down a targeted website, while others may try to include their own spam. Worse attacks might even try and trick your users to provide information or compromise user accounts.

CloudFlare has tools available to mitigate various types of attacks.

Distributed denial of service

A common attack on the Internet is the **distributed denial-of-service** (**DDoS**) attack. A distributed denial-of-service attack involves producing so many requests for a service that it cannot fulfill them, and crumbles under the load.

A common way this is handled in practice is by having the attacker make a server request, but never listen for the response. Typically a response will be presented by the client notifying the server that it received data, but if a client does not acknowledge, the server will keep trying for quite a while. A single client could send thousands of these requests per second, but the server would not be able to handle many at once.

Another twist to these attacks is the dynamic denial-of-service attack. This attack will be spread across many machines, making it difficult to tell where the attacks are coming from.

CloudFlare can help with this because it can monitor when users are trying an attack and reject access, or require a captcha challenge to gain access. It also monitors all of its customers for this, so if there is an attack happening on another CloudFlare site, it can protect yours from the traffic attacking the site as well.

It is a difficult problem to solve. Sometimes traffic just spikes if big news article are run. It is hard to tell when it's legitimate traffic and when it is an attack. For this, CloudFlare offers multiple levels of DoS protection.

On the CloudFlare settings the **Security** tab is where you can configure this advanced protection:

The basic settings are rolled into the **Basic protection level** setting:

SQL injection

SQL injection is a more involved attack. On a web page, you may have a field like a username/password field. That field will probably be checked against a database for validity.

The database queries to do this are simple text strings. This means that if the query is written in a way that doesn't explicitly prevent it, an attacker can start writing their own queries.

A site that is not equipped to handle these cases would be susceptible to hackers destroying data, gaining access by pretending to be other users, or accessing data they otherwise would not have access to.

It is a difficult problem to check against when building a software. Even big companies have had issues.

CloudFlare mitigates this by looking for requests containing things that look like database queries. Almost no websites take in raw database commands as normal queries. This means that CloudFlare can search for suspicious traffic and prevent it from accessing your page.

Cross-site scripting

Cross-site scripting is similar to SQL injection except that it deals with JavaScript and not database SQL. If you have a site that has comments, for example, an unprotected site might allow a hacker to put their own JavaScript on it. Any other user of the site could execute that JavaScript. They could do things like sniff for passwords, or even credit card information.

CloudFlare prevents this in a similar fashion by looking for requests that contain JavaScript and blocking them.

Open ports

Often, services available on a server can be available without the sysadmin knowing about it. If Telnet is allowed, for example, an attacker could simply log in to the system and start checking out source code, looking into the database, or taking down the website.

CloudFlare acts as a firewall to ensure that the ports are blocked even if the server has them open.

Challenge page

When CloudFlare receives a request from a suspect user, it will usually show a challenge page asking the user to fill out a captcha to access the site. The options for customizing these settings is on the **Security Settings** tab:

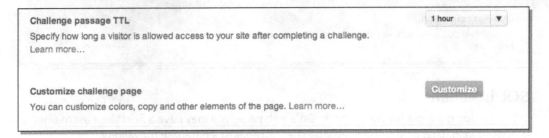

You can also configure how that page looks by clicking on **Customize**. By default, it will look something like the following:

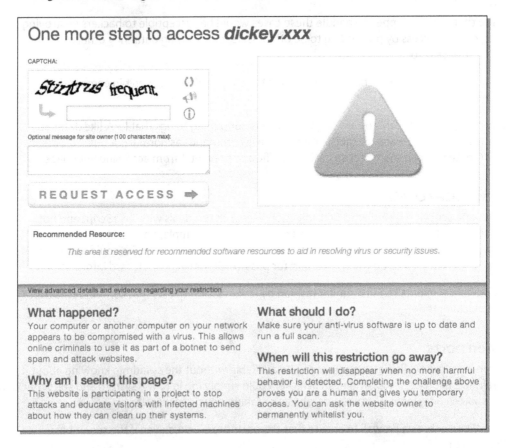

E-mail address obfuscation

E-mail address obfuscation scrambles any e-mail addresses on your page, then runs some JavaScript to decode it so that the text ends up being readable. This is nice in order to avoid getting spam in your user's e-mails, but the downside is that if a user has JavaScript disabled, they will not be able to read e-mail addresses:

Server side exclude

If there is any content you really don't want suspicious users to see, you can wrap it in the `<!—sse-->` tags to hide it:

Browser integrity check

A browser integrity check will analyze the HTTP headers to see if the user appears suspicious. I suggest enabling this as another method to look for potentially suspicious users:

Hotlink protection

Hotlink protection ensures that your images cannot be easily stolen and put on another site via hotlinks. The users will still be able to download the images and rehost them, but would not be able to use your site to do so:

The only reason to enable this would be to prevent server costs of hosting images on a high-traffic site. However, CloudFlare should optimize images, making this a somewhat minor security feature.

Threat control

The threat control part of CloudFlare allows you to see the individuals that are getting blocked and see more information about them:

Here I can see all the spammers and botnet zombies that have come to my site. By hovering over the **CHALLENGED** text, I can also see that they all had reached a captcha, but did not pass it. If I were to notice that a user was hitting the same captcha and passing it, I might want to whitelist their IP by clicking on **TRUST**.

I could also add in a range of IPs that I wanted to trust.

SSL configuration

If you have any sort of login/authentication on your website, having SSL configured is an absolutely necessary security step you will have to take.

Why SSL is important

When you access information on the Internet, the data does not flow directly to/from your computer. It actually goes out to every computer on the network and those that want the traffic pay attention. For example, when you're browsing Facebook, every single person on your Wi-Fi network is receiving the same data that your browser is. They can choose to listen to that traffic and easily pretend to be you.

SSL encrypts that traffic, so even if someone tried listening to the data, they will not be able to understand the information.

If you are unfamiliar with SSL, I highly suggest looking up the Firesheep exploit on the Internet. A couple of years ago it allowed even non-technical users the ability to almost immediately hack into someone's Facebook account just by being on the same network.

This drove Facebook to start heavily using SSL, so the issue is not nearly as severe as it once was.

On a pure content site without any login/authentication it is not necessary, however even most blog sites will have an admin login I'm sure you will want to protect.

Luckily, you're using CloudFlare, and it's very easy to set up.

[At the time of writing this book, SSL support requires the
Professional plan (or higher).]

CloudFlare Flexible SSL

Normally you will configure your server with an SSL certificate. It's a fairly involved task, and requires purchasing an expensive SSL certificate from a certificate authority. CloudFlare offers an alternative that is much simpler to set up:

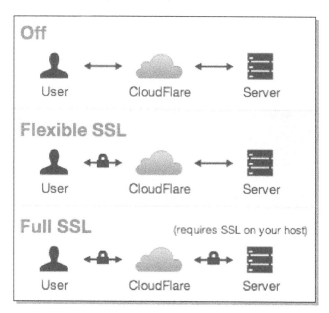

With CloudFlare, rather than ensuring that the server has an SSL connection to the user's browser, the SSL connection is only between CloudFlare and the browser. The connection between your servers and CloudFlare is unprotected.

This is usually an okay trade-off. The reason SSL is so necessary today is because of public Wi-Fi networks. The connection between CloudFlare and the server is unencrypted, but it is much less likely to have people sniffing the traffic.

Configuring CloudFlare SSL

Configuring SSL is easy with the Flexible SSL set up. Simply go to the **Settings** overview for your domain, and select the **Flexible SSL** option from the previous screenshot.

Monitoring with CloudFlare

CloudFlare offers some unique tools to be able to analyze your site's traffic. Most analytic tools work by running some JavaScript on the page. But it won't work when a browser doesn't have JavaScript, or if the user views the page too quickly for the JavaScript to notify the analytics service of an update.

CloudFlare is able to analyze all traffic because it is actually serving the traffic. It doesn't need any external JavaScript to function.

To access the analytics, click on the **Analytics** button on your website list in CloudFlare:

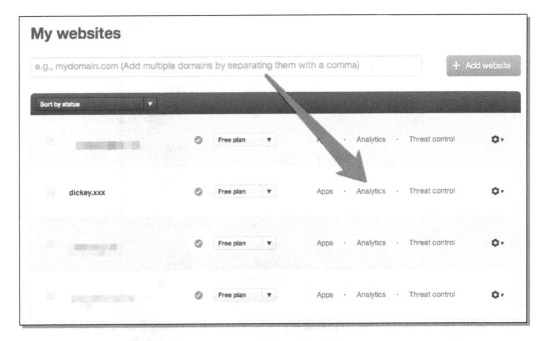

Types of traffic

From here, you'll see some graphs showing details about your traffic:

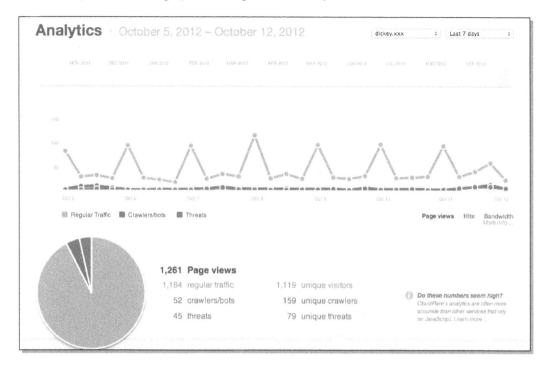

You'll notice something very different with CloudFlare if you compare it to another analytics tool such as Google Analytics. First, the numbers will be much higher. Also, it will be separating the traffic into **regular traffic, crawlers/bots**, and **threats**.

Regular traffic might be a regular user, or it might be an automated process that CloudFlare doesn't detect. You'll see on mine how every few days I get a huge traffic boost for some reason. I imagine that is because of some bot. Google Analytics uses JavaScript to track users. Because of the JavaScript-based tracking, it is not able to show that traffic from bots.

Here is Google Analytics showing the same timeframe:

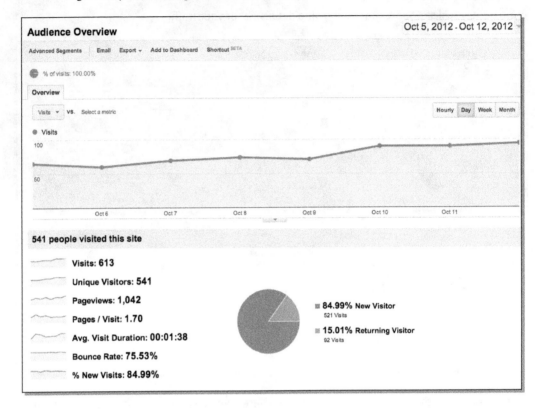

Crawlers/bots are requests hitting your site that CloudFlare does recognize as being from an automated tool. These are usually search engine crawlers that are indexing your site. They can also be bots like Facebook trying to get metadata about your site if people are sharing content. They are generally harmless. If you would like to control them more, look into the `robots.txt` file.

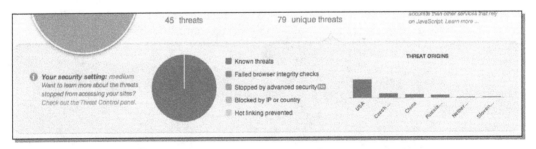

Threats are not necessarily dangerous. You will almost certainly get traffic marked as threats no matter what. CloudFlare will watch traffic it marks as dangerous as it goes around the Internet. Some of these will be poking around your site, but not necessarily doing anything malicious. Still, that traffic is best avoided. You can get a better idea of exactly who is being marked as a threat by clicking on the **Threat control** link.

This is also the section you can use to get a better idea of the repercussions of setting your security settings.

Performance

This section will show how well the performance part of CloudFlare is working. Most of the improvements will be due to CloudFlare serving JavaScript, images, and style sheets without hitting your web server. This is where you want to be looking as you tune the various performance settings. The more you can offload to CloudFlare, the better.

Search engines

This section shows how often search engines are indexing your site. More crawling is not necessarily a good thing.

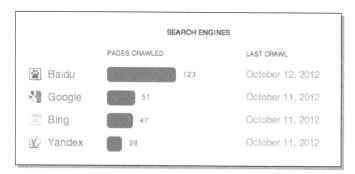

Search engines will attempt to browse around your site to find content. They will do this on a somewhat regular basis. What is better, however, is to guide them through your content. For Google, I highly recommend signing up for their Webmaster tools at `http://www.google.com/webmasters`. In the tools, they will give you hints on how to design your site to better allow crawling.

If you can set up a sitemap for the search engines, you will find that the crawl rate might reduce dramatically. This is expected, as you would now be describing where your content is and how often to check for it rather than letting the crawler figure out by itself.

Optimizing your site for a search engine is one of the best ways to get more traffic to your site. Definitely work with your search engines to find the best way to optimize your content.

Optional modules to enable and configure

CloudFlare has an extensive array of apps for you to check out. For the large majority, these apps will all work with minimal configuration, and no changes to backend code. Some of the apps are free and some are paid.

To get started, go to the **Apps** section for your domain. You can find it on your domain dashboard at the **Apps** link:

Most of these apps can be installed just by flipping the switch next to the app on this Apps dashboard.

The available apps may change after this book is published.

A Better Browser

A Better Browser will show users a warning if they are using an old version of Internet Explorer. It will also trigger if the user is operating a new browser in compatibility mode.

It can be useful if the experience for your application is not optimal in the old versions of IE such as IE6 and IE7. It will show a warning such as the following:

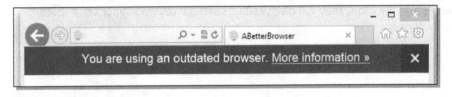

Blitz

Blitz is a load-testing tool. It can be helpful to see how your application is performing in general, or to compare it against how it runs under CloudFlare.

Note that Blitz will only perform test loading of HTML pages and not the assets on them. Most of what CloudFlare does to optimize your site is with regard to asset performance. I would only expect minor improvements (if any) when loading under Blitz.

When you run a rush with Blitz, you'll see a report such as the following:

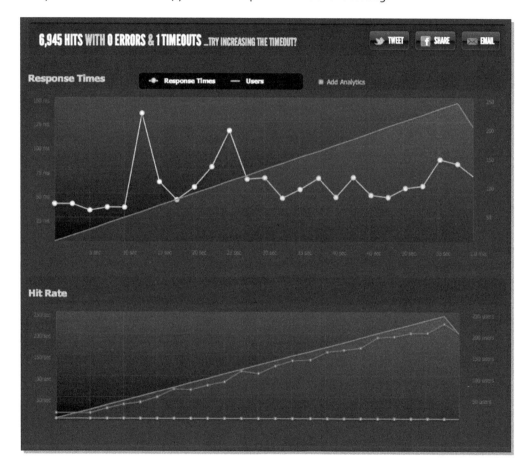

You can use that to tune your site to see how much load you can handle. Also, it's great for testing the potential for performance improvements.

cdnjs

cdnjs is a script repository containing popular JavaScripts. If you use any of the scripts at `http://cdnjs.com/`, it will help your users to use them from cdnjs. Not only do these JavaScripts run from a CDN, but they're also likely to be available on many other websites. This means that the first time a user visits your site, they will not have to download the script.

To use cdnjs, you can either edit your site to use the URL from `http://cdnjs.com/`, or just click on one of the scripts in the configuration:

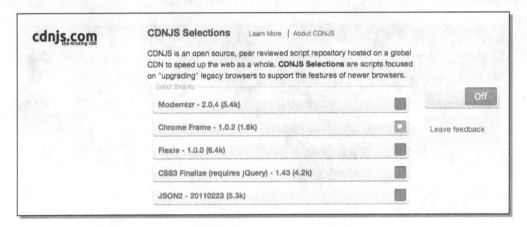

Clicky

Clicky is an analytics service that specializes in real-time traffic. It is a paid service, but can be enabled straight through CloudFlare with no configuration.

CodeGuard

CodeGaurd offers the ability to back up your site daily. It works via FTP and MySQL. It also works well with WordPress. If you have a different stack, you'll have to investigate alternate methods of backup. You'll have to enable this through your web server.

Experimently

Experimently offers heatmaps that display where users are clicking on items on your site. It can be useful to get an idea of the UX behind different parts of your site:

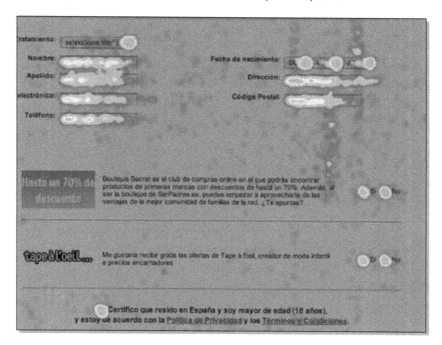

ExceptionHub

ExceptionHub tracks JavaScript errors on your site. If you use heavy amounts of JavaScript, it can give you a good idea about the problems your users may be experiencing.

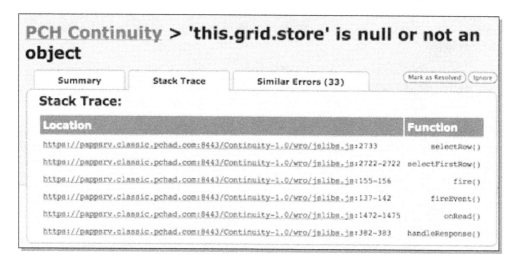

Google Analytics

The Google Analytics app will ensure that Google Analytics is correctly enabled on your site. Google Analytics is a popular, free way to measure website traffic. You can see how many users are viewing your site, where they are coming from, and what content they see. Google Analytics also has the ability to see the paths users take through your website, and where they are coming from (referrers, search, and so on):

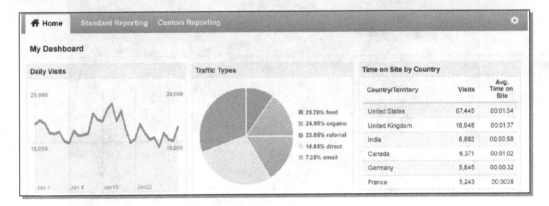

Google Webmaster Tools

The webmaster tools provided by Google can also be enabled via CloudFlare. The Webmaster Tools allow you to see how well Google and other crawlers can view your site, as well as detecting other possible issues your site might have.

Like Google Analytics, it provides some insight into where users are coming from and linking to. It shows some detail on where search comes from as well. It's designed less for analytics and more to watch out for obvious issues.

It can help you set up a site map to guide the crawler around your site, show how often the crawler is hitting your site, see what pages the crawler can access, and what pages look like to the crawler.

If you want organic search traffic, it's a good idea to check up on it every few weeks to see if there are any major issues to look at.

OpenDyslexic

Many web fonts are difficult to read for people with dyslexia. There are some fonts that can help dyslexics read sites. OpenDyslexic will enable these fonts so that dyslexic users will have an easier time reading your content.

Monitus and Pingdom

Monitus and Pingdom will keep checking your site on a regular basis to ensure that it is running. They will only be able to do that to a limited extent, such as if the front page is loading. Other issues involving logging in or database use may not be caught.

Still, it's a good idea to have an automated service checking your site regularly so that you can quickly fix any issues that may arise.

UserVoice

UserVoice puts a tab on the side of your site allowing your users to ask for help or features. If you would like to publicize your upcoming features and give a forum for users to suggest features, it is a good way to facilitate that.

Trumpet

Trumpet shows temporary messages to your users. It is helpful if you frequently need to show messages to your users but do not because you need to deploy a new code. It also allows the users to dismiss the messages after they read them.

SnapEngage

SnapEngage is a support tool that allows your users to click on a button on your site to immediately connect with you via Google Chat.

People and places you should get to know

One of the best things about CloudFlare is the wealth of helpful information, sample code, documentation, and community support around this technology. This chapter includes references to some useful resources to help you get up to speed with CloudFlare technology as quickly as possible.

Official sites

- Homepage: `cloudflare.com`
- Documentation and support: `cloudflare.com/support`
- Blog: `blog.cloudflare.com`
- Available apps: `cloudflare.com/apps`

Articles and tutorials

- How DNS works: `http://www.howstuffworks.com/dns.htm`
- How SSL works: `http://www.geocerts.com/ssl/how_ssl_works`

Twitter

- Official CloudFlare Twitter account: `https://twitter.com/CloudFlare`
- Author's Twitter account: `https://twitter.com/dickeyxxx`

Thank you for buying
Instant CloudFlare Starter

About Packt Publishing

Packt, pronounced 'packed', published its first book "*Mastering phpMyAdmin for Effective MySQL Management*" in April 2004 and subsequently continued to specialize in publishing highly focused books on specific technologies and solutions.

Our books and publications share the experiences of your fellow IT professionals in adapting and customizing today's systems, applications, and frameworks. Our solution based books give you the knowledge and power to customize the software and technologies you're using to get the job done. Packt books are more specific and less general than the IT books you have seen in the past. Our unique business model allows us to bring you more focused information, giving you more of what you need to know, and less of what you don't.

Packt is a modern, yet unique publishing company, which focuses on producing quality, cutting-edge books for communities of developers, administrators, and newbies alike. For more information, please visit our website: www.packtpub.com.

Writing for Packt

We welcome all inquiries from people who are interested in authoring. Book proposals should be sent to author@packtpub.com. If your book idea is still at an early stage and you would like to discuss it first before writing a formal book proposal, contact us; one of our commissioning editors will get in touch with you.

We're not just looking for published authors; if you have strong technical skills but no writing experience, our experienced editors can help you develop a writing career, or simply get some additional reward for your expertise.

WordPress 3 Complete

ISBN: 978-1-84951-410-1   Paperback: 344 pages

Create your own complete website or blog from scratch with WordPress

1. Learn everything you need for creating your own feature-rich website or blog from scratch

2. Clear and practical explanations of all aspects of WordPress

3. In-depth coverage of installation, themes, plugins, and syndication

4. Explore WordPress as a fully-functional content management system

Migrating to Drupal 7

ISBN: 978-1-78216-054-0   Paperback: 158 pages

Learn how to quickly and efficiently migrate content into Drupal 7 from a variety of sources including Drupal 6 using automated migration and import processes

1. Learn how to import content and data into your Drupal 7 site from other websites, content management systems, and databases

2. Upgrade your Drupal 6 site to Drupal 7 and migrate your CCK based content into the Drupal 7 fields based framework

3. Use modules that will automate the import and migration process including the Feeds and Migrate modules

Please check **www.PacktPub.com** for information on our titles